Time Travelers:

Stories of Reincarnation

Past-Life Regression Compilations

ANNA MARIA PANICI

BALBOA
PRESS
A DIVISION OF HAY HOUSE

Balboa Press books may be ordered through booksellers or by contacting:

Balboa Press
A Division of Hay House
1663 Liberty Drive
Bloomington, IN 47403
www.balboapress.com
1 (877) 407-4847

Because of the dynamic nature of the Internet, any web addresses or
links contained in this book may have changed since publication and
may no longer be valid. The views expressed in this work are solely those
of the author and do not necessarily reflect the views of the publisher,
and the publisher hereby disclaims any responsibility for them.

The author of this book does not dispense medical advice or prescribe the use
of any technique as a form of treatment for physical, emotional, or medical
problems without the advice of a physician, either directly or indirectly. The
intent of the author is only to offer information of a general nature to help you
in your quest for emotional and spiritual well-being. In the event you use any
of the information in this book for yourself, which is your constitutional right,
the author and the publisher assume no responsibility for your actions.

Any people depicted in stock imagery provided by Thinkstock are models,
and such images are being used for illustrative purposes only.
Certain stock imagery © Thinkstock.

Print information available on the last page.

ISBN: 978-1-5043-3684-0 (sc)
ISBN: 978-1-5043-3685-7 (e)

Balboa Press rev. date: 08/27/2015

Foreword: Acknowledgements

First and foremost I would like to thank and honor the Hypnosis Institute of Tarzana where I got certified as a Hypnotherapist in 2010. Because of this amazing institution that exists in Los Angeles, I was given the precious gift of hypnosis, which positively changed my life and in turn the lives of so many others. I highly recommend this for anyone considering to extend their education and deepen their knowledge of themselves.

A most gracious big Thank You from the bottom of my heart to my dear mother, Iren Panici, who supported me in this process in every way. She has been my best source of strength and drive, always encouraging me to continue my education, to be a better human being and to write books.. Mom, I did it!

Thank you to all my friends and loved one who have been on my side, who encouraged my spiritual evolution, who were patient and loving with me throughout this process of unfolding and who are still in my life by my side doing that. I love each and every one of you dearly, and couldn't have done it without you... Thank you!!

Thank you to all my clients who showed up for our hypnosis sessions, who trusted me in this process and who had the courage to go within themselves to do the deep inner healing. I am so grateful for people like you who are on the path of light, dedicated to their spiritual advancement.

Thank you to all my readers like you, who support me by buying this book and reading it, who give energy to such important matters as Reincarnation, Past-lives, Quantum healing and the possibility of time travel. I encourage you to keep up the good work and continue to dig deeper in the outer Universe, as well as in the most important place, the inner YOUniverse, where the keys to life's mysteries exist.

If you are curious to know more about your own personal story and past-life travels, I am available for bookings and to answer your questions.

Please visit my website at:

www.get-hypnotized.com

In deep gratitude and service in Love and Light,

Anna Maria Panici

From the time that I got certified as a Past-Life Regression Hypnotherapist in 2010 until today, I have personally done 145 individual past-life regressions. When I first started doing this back then, I was actually skeptical about the idea of reincarnation and past lives. I was very much into metaphysics and spirituality though, so I had an open mind about everything. I wanted to find answers for myself by experiencing things on my own, and to find actual proof that this is a real possibility. If indeed humans have lived on this planet in many various previous incarnations, as some of these theories and ancient religious beliefs state that we have, then I wanted to know answers and find truth.

Five years later, I am still taking clients through hypnosis into their past lives. Out of the 145 people, there were only 7 who were not able to see anything... most people have clear knowing, visuals and the remembrance of their names, places they lived in, dates and all the other relevant information. If it weren't for such a large number of people whom I have personally met and taken under, I might still be skeptical of the idea of reincarnation today... However, my personal data and experience have brought me to seeing and believing.

I have recently decided to compile this large amount of information and these individual stories into a book form, as to share this precious and important information with as many people as possible. The main message and purpose of this book is to share with you that Reincarnation is indeed real, that we are all connected through time, past-present-future, karma, telepathy and the unseen energy that binds us to this third dimensional time and space reality known as life on planet Earth.

The names of my clients have been changed as to protect each individual's privacy, so I have made up the names written here. The names are the only thing that I have made up, everything else is exactly transcribed from my notes as I wrote them the day of each session. I do not share my clients' personal information as I am bound by the code of ethics and morals of confidentiality in my professional business practice. Almost everyone who I did these regressions on when asked did not want to have their private stories publicly known and shared, this is why their names are not published. This is very understandable, I wouldn't want my past lives shared publicly either, unless I am discussing it in confidentiality with a friend. I do give a real vague number to their age and a vague personal description, which is for the reader to have a mental association of the present day person versus the past life personas. Also, I usually start the journey by grounding the Spirit into the body, by having them looking first at their feet, then describing what kind of shoes and clothes they are wearing, then describing their bodies, then their surroundings. That is why most journeys have a similar beginning and plotline.

Throughout the years working as a Hypnotherapist, I have learned so much from these experiences and from working with my hypnosis clients. I have grown, changed and evolved tremendously on my own spiritual path as well. In 2006 I had a massive spiritual awakening, which has guided me deeper into myself and propelled me further on my path to finding the truth of who I am beyond this human body and existence. It eventually led me to try any and every healing modalities, which then led me to get certified as a Hypnotherapist at the Hypnosis Motivation Institute of Tarzana, in Los Angeles. This was as a direct and indirect result of getting hypnosis sessions for myself in an effort to heal and transform my story and life. I wanted to be free of the past, to be a more positive, free and happy person and to manifest at ease the life that I envisioned for myself. At that time I was doing Past-Life Regressions on only a few people, as part of the training I received at HMI and because people were coming to me asking for this. I had no idea at that time that I would get so deeply involved in this and end up one day compiling all that information into a book!

Since the time I first started doing these Past-Life Regressions, I have matured and evolved a great deal, which is reflected in these documented regressions. I have learned to guide people's energy more gently and effectively, to ask the right questions that would have the most meaningful information for their current life today and to get the deep healing through taking people into forgiveness and self-love. I am now able to place the person vibrationally into the exact life that is most relevant to what the person is going through now, and guide them into the lifetime where the origin of their discomfort comes from. Painful emotions and karma and are usually released through doing the deep inner healing work of forgiveness, understanding why that life happened, and opening the heart to feeling love.

I usually take people into two or three lifetimes per session, and I document each and every one by taking notes, carefully documenting each journey and lifetime. I have a few audio recordings as well, but only do this when the client requests it. When I first started doing this, it was honestly more for the fun of it, for the money that I made from it and to appease my curiosity. I did not think that I would ever come to this point where I would be a professional therapist with an office and a full business practice... especially not doing Past-Life Regression therapy work as my main profession! I was a full time actress and model working professionally in Hollywood..... which was my desired path, goal and intention at that time. However, life is funny sometimes, it takes us to so many various, synchronistic places and so I find myself here now. Compelled by some invisible force to write and share this information with the entire world. Unfortunately, out of personal neglect in the first few years, as well as a lot of moving homes, and not knowing that my personal notes from these regressions might have value or importance someday, I do not have all of my notebooks from the first 3-4 years of doing this... What I have recuperated from all the moves and all the stories that I was given permission to share, I am now sharing with you, as it was written and recorded by me at the time of each regression. Also, English is not my first language, it is my fifth language actually, so please excuse me for any grammar errors made or for not writing more eloquently.

I now fully see the value of these stories being shared, and understand that through all these various human life-stories there emerges a common thread of humanity. Each individual story is a link and an important piece to the bigger picture and to knowing ourselves better as humans. There is also revelation of the origin of our species upon planet Earth, information on life beyond this planet in various galaxies and dimensions, information on Atlantis and Lemuria, spaceships, extraterrestrial life and prophecies of things to come in the future.

The names, dates and info pertaining to each regression are all exactly as I got them downloaded and told by each person, and this information can be nowadays easily verified by the internet or books in libraries, as pertaining to the actual people and events from the past. There is real historical and empirical evidence here because of the many dates, names and places. The people who I worked with and have done these past-life regressions on are all of different gender, ages, ethnicities, religions and come from all over the world. Most are first-timers, who are just curious about who they were in a past life. A few of these people are my friends or people who I know personally, but the majority are strangers who have found me from the magazines that I advertise in or through word of mouth.

Of course, I am not the only one who has done work and research on Past lives and Reincarnation. Edgar Cayce, Brian Weiss, Ian Stevenson and Dolores Cannon are just some of the more known and highly esteemed people who have done extensive well-documented research within this field. I invite everyone to dig deeper and do their own research about this important topic, as it is fascinating and life-changing!

Life is indeed a mystery.... Possibly the greatest mystery in the vast Universe! The question of who are we, why we are here and what is the origin of life on this planet is much more easily answered when one has access to "the other side" through hypnosis and other spiritual practices that open the door from the known physical world into the other dimensions and planes of existence. The answers are all right here, inside each and every one of us, in each and every cell of our physical body.... Our subconscious minds and DNA contain the information and memory of our history. Suffering from amnesia... humans are encoded to forget... so we feel lost by only looking to the outer world for answers to our inner world of spirit, even though we desperately seek to know WHO we are, WHY we are here and HOW we can change our lives for the better. This is where we can find the answers to questions that science has not been able to answer yet... and collectively piece together the puzzle of humanity's lost history.

Joseph, 30's Middle Eastern man. October 2011

Life #1

Man with boots on, in his mid 30's, his name is John Montgomery........has a farm where he plowed on the field............there is a house behind him, wife and daughters........in the US, mid 1800's. He is frustrated by not growing corn and wheat, owns his land. Springfield is the nearest town. He is not interested in family, only in the field and building the farm. He is a strong man, experienced in life. Has no real connection with his wife, doesn't have many friends. Does not read very well, has basic training and schooling

*Plus 10 years into the future: He is in a town, in Winchester. Shopping….. at a bar…. Works in a mercantile shop. He is not happy with his own life, because it didn't work out well……. His wife doesn't love him. Has 2 daughters, but no relationship with them…….. He is mad at God and the weather. He is not religious, is a simple man. The year is 1826.

*Death transition: He is in a jail cell, sick. He shot someone, for money. He didn't care that he killed someone, is depressed and miserable because "things didn't work out"

Life #2

Has boots on, shiny and comfortable........male...........
crisp and fresh air, sees the ocean and the sky...... In
Europe maybe. "Aquadran", before the planet was
populated.

There are others in the group, they are missionaries from
a different planet "ZX"....they are human-like, came from
"Pananopia" star system. They came to earth to populate
it because their own planet is overpopulated. They want to
grow their kind...... social interactions and experiments
will take place........ There are no other humans on earth
yet, the human race started from their race, it is the same

There are animals on earth, haven't seen them yet...
they brought figs and other fruit variations from their
planet. There is a space station in the stratosphere, they
came down through a pod......he is great at organizing.
Part of the mission is to populate earth. He is excited
about the mission! They monitor earth in the future, to
understand themselves better, to populate the universe
and what they know. They have advanced computer
systems. The spaceship travels fast, is made of a metallic
substance, bends and forms, is pliable. Earth doesn't have
such materials. He took some sample rocks. No food.
He is only allowed to come down to earth once, limited
regulation. He saw the ice caps from the pod. They are
here to learn from themselves, to populate earth with not
much......no pyramids or anything formed here yet at
that time. They want to leave no trace, no signs of them
having ever been here, as to have a "pure experiment".
They are volunteers from their planet. He has parents

back home and a brother…. It is very honorable for him to leave.

He is a man in his 20's, dark hair, strong and fit. He is excited, taking part of creation of another world. Wants to stay but can't. Travels by spaceship…. It's like a small city, there are restaurants and shops.

The planet is graphed out into 32 main quadrants………. their scientists used hybrids to create new ones to see how they perform.

He is not afraid of anything, he is excited, wants to meet a girl. Has a life expectancy of 60-80 years. "XZynea" is the name of their planet………they populate other planets as well…….. life is hectic and busy on his planet, but there are no wars, because they entered the age of "Advanced Enlightenment"……. He finds this boring, but it works

*Plus 20 years into the future: Married, lives back on his own planet…….it's crowded, fast and busy. He is happy now, but misses the experience of traveling to other planets. Hs a son and a daughter, a decent job and home, everyone gets along. The city he lives in is called "Suria"

*Death transition: In bed in a hospital…..his family is there, his children are around him. He is back on his own planet. He is dying of old age, 86 years old…. He would have liked to be involved in bigger things. He feels loved.

Jeremy, 33 years old, Caucasian man. March 2012

Life #1

Naked man, alone, Ezekiel, 30's…………... sand, the ocean all around him, in Africa or Egypt……looking for his family…..was on a ship, there was a storm and he was washed ashore…… came from Spain, was traveling to provide for his family, as a fisherman

*Plus 5 years into the future: In a village, Caldonia (Spain)……….reunited with his family: wife, daughter, son…….Life's purpose: to serve his family. Wants a happy, simple life

*Death transition: Daughter next to him, at home…….. dying of old age. Has no regrets. Most valuable lessons learned: spend as much time with his family as possible, and to love more.

Life #2

Little boy, 6 years old, Irish. Jonathan. People around him…. In New York, mom is pregnant…. Going to school, baseball is his favorite hobby.

*Plus 10 years into the future: In the country, driving by himself……….has a girlfriend…….is on the run from the

cops because he robbed a bank to support his family. The purpose of his life: to grow and evolve.

*<u>Death transition</u>: In a hospital….56 years old, dying of lung cancer. Regrets smoking, and not having children. Forgives himself.

Jake, mid 20's, Caucasian man. May 2012

Life #1

Has shiny shoes, brown vest on, with a collar shirt and a neck tie......slacks on, old-fashioned attire, has a pocket watch................. 30 years old, name is "Albert Tein" or "Al". He is in charge of a business or saloon, managing it. 1865, Southwest America. He has big, manly hands, from mining.........mines for gold, as a hobby, it's his passion. He understands visualization, and finds gold after "seeing it" in his dreams and mind. He keeps gold as a collection. Is not married, doesn't want to be. He likes his present situation, and doesn't feel a connection to his own family... he left them behind. He is searching for a new movement, an idea..... Love and happiness, abundance and security, to create his own family. He desires children in the future.

*Plus 20 years into the future: Beautiful house on the side of the mountain, there is a gathering of family and friends. He is cooking the meat that he hunted earlier, quail and deer. Laughing with friends, has a family now. He is highly respected in the community, his children are teenagers and he is proud of them. Wife is "Margaret", has dark, curly hair. He is retired from work. Lives in the Mexico territory. He is happy with his life and feels fulfilled. Wants to travel with his wife and watch his children grow and mature.

*Death transition: By a waterfall, he is 88 years old. God sick and requested to die by a waterfall. He is old and ready to die. His wife and friends are there, with his sons and grandsons.

Paul, mid 40's Caucasian man. June 2012

Life #1

Bare feet, shorts or a loin cloth, man…. Is young and strong, 15 years old, his name is "Radha" good looking, and strong. In Egypt, around 4,000 years ago….. Has a family: mother, father, 3 brothers and 2 sisters. In a desert…. There are huts, people working. He is in a field, farming, goes to school… and sees himself now getting taken or stolen away by women and strong men, gets put in a blanket and into a cart. Is scared…. He is taken away, and is angry. He has no way to escape, so he has to accept his life and where he is. He is 18 years old now. Was brainwashed in his sleep, and broken into being a slave. He was sleep deprived and hungry a lot. Usual food was: lamb and veggies and fruits. He tried to escape there, but couldn't…

He sees the Queen "Sangha" she has light eyes and dark hair. He is either a servant and a slave…… seeing pyramids. He is at the Queen's feet, on his knees, he belongs to her. He feels ok about it now, is confident, and likes belonging to her. He makes her drinks and cleans. He tried to escape at first, then she trained him to stay………through various violent and mind-control methods. There is no king, just slaves all around and women. In a big palace, somewhere in Cairo.

*20 years into the future: The Queen gave him away, as a reward. He is now in a bigger palace. He likes being under

8

someone's control, it's all he knows, and is comfortable being taken care of….. His goals and dreams: to please the Queen and do his duty well.

*Death transition: In a dungeon atmosphere, he had an injury… is not useful anymore, so they put him away and left him. 51 years old.

Life #2

Body feels heavy………Roman times, after Christ. He is a soldier on a horse. Has armor and a sword. He doesn't like being a soldier, or battles or fighting. Wants peace and to not fight. He came from a family where his father, grandfather and uncle were all soldiers, so he had to be a soldier too. He was a sensitive child, but had to be tough, was taught to be hard. 25 years old, in Rome, Italy. His name is "Dante", is married and has 3 children. Has to go on patrol for weeks at a time. He is fighting the rebels from different villages and territories, keeping them checked and in line. He has killed many people, he doesn't like it, but has to. Sort of like a police officer. Some of his comrades enjoy torturing people. He wants to move away and be a farmer, be with his family and children, but he can't escape the Roman empire….

*Death transition: He is ambushed and killed by a mob of people. 34 years old. He gave love to his family, and wishes that he could have been able to break free and out of that soldier lifestyle and move away.

Douglas, mid 30's Caucasian man. July 2012

Life #1

Orange glow, surrounded by moving energy.... Like wings, moving up and down.... Feels like floating. Sees a black hole... its purpose is to transcend Energy, to move it from one place to another. He is in transition.

Sunlight now... like a fog.......he has no physical body, is just energy. In a different dimension. Is by himself, in a place "lost"

Life #2

Body feels heavy... Man... drifting, feels powerful, but helpless. Strong, feels his hands, not his feet. Feels glowing energy, at the edges........ his hands feel like globes of energy, he is sending energy out through them. He is always learning and evolving, and is preparing himself for the work ahead. Feels amazing energy.

He is getting downloads and messages to: continue on the path. At the beginning, reached a void of nothingness, is just energy. In a state of comfort, is attempting to understand it, being it.

The light moves like clouds, but can't come through... because of the darkness.... The nothingness, is the state of in between.

Josh, early 40's, Caucasian man. August 2012

Life #1

Man, has leather flip flops on………. Is in his mid 20's,has a beard, is stocky and medium built, has leather archer gear on, in a forest. Is hunting, or on guard… on the lookout. The year is 1642, in England. He is missing someone, his love…. Her name is "Marianne", but they are not supposed to be together because they are in different casts. He is missing her very much and is concerned. His family is dead, was murdered by the king. He is sad about it, took it very tragically and has a heartache. He created freedom in work. The lesson for him: be present, don't hold on to any expectations of the future….. live, love and let go.

*Death transition: Dying of natural causes, died content at 42. Surrounded by people who loved him.

Life #2

Barefoot, his feet are calloused and worn out. He is indigenous, in Mexico. Sees temples, culture, no year measured. He is a man, doing healing and shamanic work, is a lightworker. 22 years old. He learned from the head shaman, as part of his family lineage. There was a battle between the use of energy and the manipulation of it, between a few groups in the community who want control and to sacrifice people, in the name of "the Light".

In the future he sees himself having a wife that is of royal status, is in love, but needs to protect and take care of. Is dressed in tribal clothing, with bands of leather and bare skin. His lesson: can't stop what will happen, this is bigger than him.

*Death transition: Gets his heart ripped out by human sacrifice ritual. The whole culture falls apart and gets destroyed.... By foreigners, who have headgear on and lots of fabric and metals. They kill off people.

Jessica, early 30's Jewish woman, August 2012

Life #1

Seeing a small boat, wooden… sees water in a Bay. Old man named "Isaac", 60 or 70 years old, who uses the boat for fishing, and fishes alone always. He feels like he is drowning or floating in the water… getting deeper and deeper in the water, being pulled down by his heavy robe and is tangled, is breathless and dies.

Life #2

Is in a jungle with trees, it's wet and tropical, somewhere in South America. He is dark skinned, with brown legs and arms, 12 years old. Is in a ceremony or tribal ritual, with people of his tribe all around him, but he can't see them… He was told to do this by a member of his group. Is feeling nauseous and has a headache, sees a vision of a snake and a bird…. The bird is carrying the snake.

*Death transition: He is laying in the dirt, where he goes to sleep at night…. Is coughing and can't breathe….. many people of his group have this. Releases and feels peaceful.

Matt, mid 60's, Caucasian/European man. December 2012

Life #1

The body feels like in heaven.…..sees light all around……..
the picture of him drowning in the ocean in Africa…….
He is now flying around with the angels…. They are
white, bright. He is there because it's natural, and there
is so much joy, in the 5th Dimension.

When he was 2-3 years old, he almost drowned in a pool,
saw his Spirit float away in space.

Message from the angels: he drowned in a past life, but
in this life he didn't drown because he has healing work
to do.

He is ready to step into it now.….. releasing the fear of
failure: embarrassment, shame, abandonment, betrayal….
Are the primary wounds that he is healing.

Peter, early 40's, Caucasian man, May 2014

Life #1

Has boots on and a long white robe. Man, around 80 years old, a "Centaur" ……..feels good, there are villagers all around him, looking at him……. He is a priest, teacher or a magician, sitting up on top of a hill. He was trained by the elders to do this, since he was 12 years old. He has a family, wife and 2 daughters, they are back home in the castle….. a home made of big heavy stones, on top of a hill, overlooking the valley, looks majestic. He is happy with his life. The year is 1813 in Europe. He is a philosophy teacher. His advice: Be kind to each other, and be kind to yourself. Love more, play more…. Relax, everything is ok.

*Death transition: Wife and daughters and the king are in the room. Dying of old age, but is happy… lived a full life. His favorite part of being alive were his friends, family and the love he felt.

Life #2

Has leather shoes on, with socks. Man, 23 years old, is in a University class room, studying matter and energy. His name is John Maxwell. In the US, East Coast (Phyladelphia…?) in 1946. He is English. He is in a tall, brick building on a beautiful campus… summertime. He is fascinated by energy, and is trying to prove some theory. His mother is alive in France, his father is dead. He wants to teach, be a teacher.

*<u>Plus 10 years in the future</u>: Lives in the same town, is married, has a boy and a girl. Works for his wife's father's company (chemical), has a simple, boring life.... He is not very ambitious. The purpose of this life: is to have and experience a family.

*<u>Death transition</u>: In the hospital in New York, 56 years old. Dying of lung cancer, from the chemicals from his work place. He regrets leaving his family behind, feels too young to die. His wife is there with him. Last message before dying: life is short, live every day like your last.

Elizabeth, early 30's Caucasian woman, May 2014

Life #1

*Golden toe rings, red toe polish........woman, late 20's. Has golden garments, dress and a crown on...... 14th Dynasty.... Cairo..... There is gold everywhere. "Isis" Sitting in a chair, in a palace on a throne..........there is gold everywhere, Egypt's gold. She is holding space.... Sitting in silence, like a statue..... has a bright and powerful energy inside. Feels sad and lonely, because her role is to hold space in silence, but she wants to move and interact more. Her every action is watched and recorded. The Pharaoh is not there, she feels disconnected from him. The keepers of the scrolls watch her very closely. She feels the presence of a man, the librarian, who is a friend to her and her teacher......he is teaching her sacred knowledge and secrets, about the pyramids and their blueprints. He comes from a lineage of wisdom keepers from generations and generations. The channelings of the pyramids come from a greater species, not related to humans. They have spoken to her before in temple space, in meditation they connect with her. Her role: keeper of the laws of the ancients..... Sacred feminine.... Ritual through dance, ceremony, flower-bath ceremonies, purification. She is not fully human, has mixed DNA.......... There is a great danger, and the fear of being found out, because of the greed and abuse of power...................She has 2 children, but doesn't get to see them often, they are taken care of and bred to be in power. She has a sense of duty and is not able to play with her children and family.

She writes in hieroglyphs, symbols...... There are several pyramids erect, she goes in them and prays.... Prayers to the sun, golden light, very masculine energy. Also to "the Goddess". There are crystals in the pyramid and symbols, and the sun, and lots of gold.

She feels at peace, excited and nourished. All the pyramids link up and shoot out like laser beams through the top, for the "Star Beings" to bring them energy... the "Lunai" or "Alunai"

She has wings depicted, because she is a bridge between the human race and this more advanced race. She has the ability to guide people upwards, to higher realms. She works with the feminine.

In the pyramids they are the golden balls of light, they connect the grids together...... 7, 11 or 13 women, maidens from the palace, who have some special imprint or link in their DNA.....

Advice for future humans: There is a big golden sculpture of a cat in the Pyramid of Light "Akara"......study the ancient languages and know them. Fire... used with gold as a purification ritual. Women must return to the power of the womb, connecting this energy with the stars "golden belly". Work with the sun's energy and fire for transformation.

*Death transition: looking out from a window at the pyramids. She is over 100 years old, close to 200 years.... She is choosing to die, her spirit leaving the body now.

Danielle, mid 30's Caucasian woman, July 2014

Life #1

Woman, 20 years old. Looks similar to herself now, but is wider. Has long blonde curly hair. Has a thin, flowy white dress on, with flowers and bare feet. Her name is "Tamara" she is there by herself, standing in the forest, in the sun...... There are tents, tipis, all around. The town is called "Bakti" in the country of "Zenia" on the "Tarazdan" continent, on "Naalii" planet, in the "Saspanton" galaxy. Culture: tribal, community, sharing, abundant, generous, music, ceremonies, nature loving. She does energy work with pregnant women, she has 1 child, a girl who is with her dad. They are ceremonially married, in love and happy all the time. There are no negative emotions on that planet, no death or sickness. There are animals around, they don't eat them, but play with them. They eat the vegetation. A few thousand live on this planet. They are aware of life on other planets, they visit in spaceships and other teleporting devices. She once went to another planet called "Deli", to get seeds. The purpose of life on planet "Naalii" is to build community and family. They are Nalinese and have a human fairy body type, tribal, triangular foreheads, have crystals in them, to absorb light. There is no moon on the sky at night. Life is peaceful, gentle, light and free. They want to experience divine love in symbiotic union.

Advice for humans on planet earth: There are nutrients in the soil.

Life #2

Little girl, 7 years old. She is barefoot with a nightgown on, ruffles with pink sleeves and white. She is in a building, a house...... 1902........Cine, Venezuela........ Her name is "Melissa Talc". At night, her parents are outside.... crying and screaming........ because she is in the house and it's on fire........ she died in the house, because she got suffocated. She had to teach her parents about love, that she is never gone, always there, that she exists in their hearts as love. They needed this lesson because they asked for a revelation. She contacts them through energy.

Life #3

Stones, large stone formations........in Transilvania. Man, late 30's...........has a muscular and hairy body. His name is "Dara" "Salom"...........1915. He is scrapping something, carving in the rock, to remember something......the picture of a sun and the pineal gland, with rainbow coming out of it, with 26 rays. Someone told him about this, an alien visitor. He had an encounter, was friendly, and it happened when he was meditating on a cliff.... A spaceship landed behind him, and just one being came out of it. A rusty colored, soft, like a statue, had 3 extended bone cheeks/gills...... Came from "Manu", from the "Celepsi" galaxy. Why?? They have a message for all of humanity: To live in the light, without fright. They told him that he would find truth, that love is the only thing there is, it is all of existence. If he loves deeply, he will see many colors. Drink crystal water, and to charge water with quartz crystals, and amethyst, to open the mind.

This experience has positively influenced his life, he was on a pilgrimage and decided to return back to his family after this. He developed his trade to help people, by holding that in his heart.........He performs crystal baptisms, a lot of people are coming to him for that. He chose a life of service. He is happy being of service, but feels a little empty, has no wife or girlfriend. He is Arabic nationality, and speaks that language.

*Death transition: by the stone walls. He is very old, dying of lack of affection.

James, mid 50's Caucasian man, August 2014

Life #1

Is in pure energy form, has no body… is a lightbody with energy form. Is a Rainbow Dragon, female. Flying above Maui, the heart chakra of the planet. The purpose: being a part of the creation of the heart chakra on Maui, before there was life on it. Feeling others around, and does not feel alone… there are other lightbody dragons, working together. They are pure energy, self-less, feels like passion and love… the "me" is being connected to "it" being in the energy. Receiving mother earth and father sky, working as an orchestra, in concert with each other, being in the flow. The purpose, the focus is being divinely guided. Something important is being seeded……….. This is exciting…… Not knowing…. But knowing by being…………. "Seeding" the energy for the greater energy to transform later……….. All life blossoms within the heartbeat…………..Universal transformation……… 30,000 years BC-100,000 years BC. Comes from a whole other energetic constellation, where the energies were completely pristine……. There was pure creation, pure light. All raw and uninterrupted.

Darkness……… earth, birthing, dense in the body, creates the soil for things to grow. Male/female energy……..Male is empowered, female is allowing and open. Our natural state, to come into concert.

Question: "Why me? Why do I feel the way that I do and my mission?"

Answer: "Because you can, and because you want to. This comes from before thought, you can't comprehend. Go with that and see where it takes you.... Everywhere. I am with you always. In the love between us, in all the truth that you will every know. There is nothing that you will ever have to remember, because you are done. In every moment of every day, I am with you in every way. Love's rainbow magic has begun, as it never stopped beginning"

Eva, late 20's Caucasian woman, November 2014

Life #1

Woman, 21 years old. Has a red gown on and red slippers, has long dark hair. Is in the garden outside at her home by herself.... The garden has a pool, the house looks like a castle, from old Latin times. She is married, her husband is at war. Rome, Italy, 1584. Her name is "Rebecca Brode". She is lonely all day, and is far away from her family..... She is the Queen, her husband the King of the country. She wants to have children and not feel lonely....she loves her husband "Arthur", but he is so far away and she is sad about it. He has a gold with purple crown and is tall.

*Plus 20 years into the future: Sitting at a dining room table, same house. She is by herself again, her husband is not there.... She is lonely and has no children. She loves to swim at the pool in the house and river. She has friends, but doesn't see them very often.

*Death transition: In a bed, pretty room. She is 68 years old, her husband and friends are there, and one son. She regrets not leaving the house more often and spending more time with her husband.

Life #2

Has blue boots on, a worn-in simple cotton dress with a white collar. She is a 14 year old girl, on her parents' farm with a horse. She has blonde hair with bangs, is happy, and her name is "Chelsea Deany". She goes to school with the other farm kids, and loves to ride horses. She likes a boy, "Mark", he brings her apples to school. She wants to be a teacher when she grows up and write a book.

*Plus 10 years into the future: She is 24 years old, married on the farm with a little house on it. She just had a second miscarriage, is very upset and sad about it. She is married to "Mark", the boy from her childhood. She really loves him, they are in love and live in the house that he built. Her parents are gone, she works on the farm and raises crops, tobacco... but still wants to be a teacher. She wrote a book, about a girl's life on a farm, but didn't finish it yet.... Her husband wants her to finish it and get it published, but she stopped writing after her father died, because of grief and sadness.

*Death transition: She is out on the field by herself, riding a horse, had an accident and fell off... is 28 years old. Mark is very sad....

(This is where I had her reverse time to the beginning of the day, and had her stay in at home instead of going out into the field, thus avoiding the accident and death. She had a lot of life-force energy and I felt intuitively guided to "change" the course of events to where she avoided death and lived on, thus living out her dream and love, and finishing the book she started)

*New death transition: She is 62 years old, has children and grandchildren all around her. There are apples and notes from her students all around. She finished writing her book, although didn't get it published yet... She had 5 children and a very happy, but simple life.

Chelsea, early 30's Caucasian woman, November 2014

Life #1

Male, 12 years old, his name is "Michael". He is in a small city or market, by himself. He is working, or playing…. In Florence, Italy in the 1700's. His favorite thing is running by the river. Feels abandoned sometimes… wants to be a banker when he grows up.

*Plus 10 years into the future: There is a woman with him in a home…. He works with coins. Is in love with her, thinks she is the most beautiful woman in the world, her name is "Mary" or "Magdalene". They have 2 children, are married and want to travel and explore and to give his children a better life. He is running away from the fear of his past….he worked for someone in the past who was mean or dark, was abusive with him when he was young, 10 years old, when he was left there by his caretaker. The man is big, strong and mean.

*Death transition: in a small house in the country-side, 72 years old. Advice to himself: love more, give more and be more generous with others.

Jennifer, mid 30's Caucasian woman, November 2014

Life #1

Man, has sandals on and a beard….. Is in an old hut house, sitting by a candle at a table, writing. He is a writer, and likes it. His name is "Shalom", he is from the Middle East, was looking at the moon, scientifically…. Is writing a calendar or scientific observation about it. In BC times, very long time ago… He was a nomadic shepherd in his younger years, had a caravan of people…. Going to search for food and shelter. He is not a part of that tribe anymore. He is not feeling lonely or regretting anything.

*Death transition: in the same hut structure, on a straw bed, by himself, dying of old age. Feels alone now.

Life #2

Flat shoes on… Woman, middle aged, named "Shandah". Has a daughter holding her leg, lives in Detroit, 1966. She is a housekeeper… has to do it to make money, but doesn't like it. The father of her child is absent, he is somewhere else, ill in bed…. She is in her early 40's, and would like to be a secretary in an office. Her favorite thing to do is to play with her daughter,

*Plus 5 years into the future: She is a widow now, still cleaning houses. This is a hard lessons. She is always a little angry, because she had it so hard. She is depressed,

has self-love but is frustrated with her life circumstances. Advice: have faith and better yourself to have a better situation... can change life's circumstances by believing in yourself more. She wants to do something more for her daughter "Magpie", who is always looking out of the window.

*Death transition: she is pushing a cart on the street on the sidewalk with groceries in it, is 70 years old, has a heart attack. Her daughter is moved out, and is not close to her as she would have liked it to be.

Life #2

Man, is less than 40 years old. He is on a cliff or edge, overlooking a great desert in the Western US. His nickname is "Steals Goat", as a joke. He is a funny man, but is supposed to be serious. He feels isolated and alone on this cliff, was sent there by his family and tribe to figure things out..........There is a dog next to him.......
Around the 16th Century. He wears a loincloth, is Native American, "Erakoi".... His family is in good standing, and raised him to be a serious healer, not a funny jokester that he is..... he is also not supposed to get married, or fall in love, was raised to be a shaman/healer who doesn't fall in love, but is serious. He feels constrained that his life is pre-determined..... He loves playing with his dog/ wolf most. It's raining now and it's cold outside, and he is resentful that he was sent here. He would like to just walk away and live apart from the politics and drama of the community, but he doesn't see a choice.... So he grieves a lot........... Mediating now, receives a message: it's ok to be who he is, but also he needs to be stronger.

*Plus 10 years into the future: he is sitting in a group around the camp fire, telling some kind of story: he is predicting the future, sees a vision of the future in a few hundreds of years ahead, a man in a business suit with a brief case, and tall buildings and big cities. The information is all in his head, he sees this as a vision.... They all laugh at him and this vision, because they can't believe this to be ever happening. This seems funny to him as well, but sees it very clearly. He maintained his sense of humor, but also stepped into his leadership role............. Then he sees himself dancing in a ceremonial dance, wearing the fur of his dog/wold who died. People are dancing and celebrating, like a ceremony.

*Death transition: He is inside a tipi tent, people are talking to him…. He is on a bed of straw, dying of old age, in his 80's. He feels a little bit lonely, because he didn't have anyone close to him other than his dog/wolf. He thinks back and likes most that lonely time he was in the desert by himself with his dog/wolf.

Darrel, mid 20's African American man, August 2014

*This client had a persistent sharp pain in this left side which has been bothering him for the past 4 years. He thought this might be Chakra or energy related, so he came to see me to possibly clear away karma from a past life to ease the physical discomfort he was feeling.

Life #1

Sees a woman with a headdress on... his wife..... Isis..... sees pyramids. He is Pharaoh. He is laying down.....

Life #2

Trees.....in Belgium, 1826...... Woman, 39 years old, walking by herself. Her name is "Maryam Cartan" (or Carthan, or Karthan...), she is married with children. Her family is in the house in the forest. She fishes with her husband for a living...... she wants to leave this place and go to New York to be a butcher.

*Plus 10 years into the future: She has white hair, blue eyes, thin body. She is sitting on a bed, in New York. She is sick, and couldn't feel her legs. Her family is with her. She remembers... that a train derailed a couple years ago.... her legs got hurt in the train accident. She can 't walk now. It was determined that it was the conductor's fault for the accident... The conductor is connected to the pain her side, when the train fell over on her legs. She has forgiven him, but not herself for this accident.

(*At this time in the regression I guided him through a special healing and forgiveness energy release, where he did choose to forgive herself in the past life and as this happened, the pain in his side literally lifted and left from his body. As this happened, a 3-5 inch spiral vortex opened up in the middle of my office opposite from the client, and appeared to absorb or somehow manipulate the energy of the client that he was releasing… this lasted about 5 seconds. This incident was extremely shocking and miraculous to me, as I have never in my life before or after experienced such a phenomenon. The pain in his side completely left his body after the session and has not returned since then.)

Shannon, mid 20's Caucasian woman. August 2014

Life #1

Man, 36 years old. Has sandals on and a cloth around his waist. He is outside, herding sheep on a field, they are his sheep. "Augustine"...... in the Middle East, in 732 AD. He is not married, but wants to have a family. He reads, is outside, sings.

*Plus 10 years into the future: He is married, with 2 children. He is happy, doesn't want to change his life.

*Death transition: He is in bed, with his friends and family by his side. He is dying of old age, 78 years old.

Life #2

Barefoot, has a red dress on. Is thin, has a pale face and body, 19 years old. Her name is Elizabeth Francis. She is in a garden, picking flowers. There are other people around her, but they are all far away. England in the 1700's. She is in her parent's home, they are wealthy lords. She has a good life, but is bored. She wants to go out and explore the world, to see how other people live. Her parents are very protective and want her to marry a young man.... Someone she doesn't love. She is in love with someone already, "Robert"... but he doesn't have a lot of money. Her dream is to be with him, and get away from there and her life, to go explore and see the world and be free.

*Plus 10 years ahead in time: She is in the same place, married to the man her family chose for her. This is a cold marriage, has 2 daughters, who she loves. Her new last name is "Whitaker" or "Widdecker". They live outside of London. She has traveled to London and Paris.

Her advice: follow your heart and listen to yourself, because you might end up very miserable.

*Death transition: In her bed, her 2 daughters and maids and husband are by her side. She is sick of some disease, 52 years old.

Jackie, early 30's Middle Eastern-American woman, August 2014

Life #1

Has pointy Indian shoes on, with silver thread. The year is 1903. Woman, girl… 14 years old, is small, tiny stature. She is Asian looking, in a tropical country, in Indonesia. Her mom is in the kitchen, her dad is in the temple garden, she has an older brother. She doesn't go to school…. Wants to take care of her parents.

*Plus 10 years ahead in time: She sees trees, a forest. She has 2 children and is married. Her husband is there. She paints flowers, and is happy with her life.

*Death transition: She is in a garden, in a wheelchair. She is old, 87 years old, dying of something to do with her lungs. She has no regrets.

Life #2

Man, has shoes on. Is very tall, with big wide shoulders. His name is Howard, he is in his 30's. There are lots of people in the street. It is an old city, made of brick, with steeples. In Europe in the 1800's. He is waiting to meet someone….. Is not married yet, because he hasn't fallen in love yet. He makes gloves for a living, as his work. He likes his job. His biggest dream is to find love. He does not love himself, because he is so tall, he feels unworthy. He does not have friends. He loves being able to create with his hands.

Jonas, mid 30's Caucasian man, August 2014

Life #1

In a jungle by a beach. Has blue shoes on, or blue feet......
Is standing alone. He is there to have fun and play around.
Sees a structure in the distance that is a housing building
for other people/Beings. He doesn't "see" himself, maybe
because he is not human.......the year doesn't matter, he
can go anywhere.... To a different time.... He can time
travel..... by dropping in and tuning in into the vibrations
of the Universe, the same way as traveling through space.

Feeling/sensing/loving mind.... The heart travels
through time. He chose this location. It's time-less. There
are oceans and waves.... The architecture doesn't have a
shape to it. Costa Rica maybe, or somewhere in Central
America.... On the Pacific side. Can choose to manifest a
different body, at will. He has a body now, a blue body. Is
female gender, with blue skin.... Wearing khaki colored
clothing..... "Jungle native"......Does not eat food.......
getting nourishment from the chlorophyll in his/her skin.
Takes energy from love. Is "in the future", from a different
place... is a mixture of human and spirit, from the 4th and
5th Dimension..... a combination of celestial and biological
energies that have created this incarnation. He earned
this, and chose this existence..... is completely harmonized
with life, and can live as long as he wants to..... is in tune
with the Universe. Has no fear of death........ goes with
the flow and waves......loves everything that he looks
at, he feels their love and they feel his.........Is having

different experiences all at the same time. The feeling/ sensing feels like an expression of love.

Advice to himself: It's not wrong to want what you want, and that others want other things….. To move into the direction of his future self as future Native Self, and keep evolving that way. Don't criticize other people's intelligence, because they are the entire Universe, and what it has learned until then. Don't get caught up in other people's consequences. Focus on the learning and team-work, not on the surface things.

Advice for me (the Hypnotherapist): trust that the deepest pain I am experiencing is a crucible for which energy is exchanged. You experience of it is serving the entire Universe. Don't doubt that it's the right thing to be happening. This is the experience you get to transform, and you will do it.

Advice to humans: you are exactly where you need to be, you can't go any faster. Each beat of the heart matters, in and out.

To travel through time we must learn to shift and transcend time. Being human is very special and important. We are a microcosmic version of the process. If our importance is at the expense of another Being's (nature, animals, people) then we are missing the point. We are working for the Universe and it is working for us. It loves us and respects us…….the love is evident in that we get to exist now in human form. No one is punished……. Everyone is learning at different speeds. Open your heart and feel! You know what to do…. Be open. Also open your mind, to think and feel and let everything through. Honor the human race through your actions. Open to everything you feel….. which is total body joy and feeling good.

Angela, mid 20's Caucasian woman, August 2014

Life #1

Is in a home, wearing a bonnet and a long dress. Sees children everywhere, they are hers. She is in her 40's.....
"Isabelle Granoak"............in the US, on the East Coast, in North Carolina, in "Riverdale" (the town had a few name changes), in 1742. Her husband "John", is out there fighting, for freedom against the British. She does not support it, likes her quaint country lifestyle. She is not happy with her life, feels very sedentary....... She wants to be out, roaming and seeing the world. She does love her children, but is yearning for more. Has 10 children, 2 of which died in childbirth. For work, she wants to stitch her quilts, for other people..... to create pretty, intricate designs...... She does not know "what's out there" or what's possible.

Her advice: Always look out for what's better... what you think could be. Just look within and you will find your treasure, and your peace.

*Death transition: Is laying in bed.... 74 years old, is dying of pneumonia. She has no regrets, and wants to forgive her husband for leaving as long as he did and for him being distant.

Life #2

Is a baby boy, crying. His mom is holding him, or a midwife….. Is just being born…. Sees the umbilical chord. Is in a dark room, or a shed. He came out early, because they needed him….

*Plus 5 years into the future: He is walking down the street, is very proud. His name is "Alexander Wright", lives in London in 1859. He was adopted by a wealthy couple. He is angry, because his parents are stuck up people…. His adoptive father is a banker, his adoptive mother organizes lunches and tea, they are of high society. They couldn't have children of their own, so they adopted him. He uses his gifts to play the violin. At home things are edgy… he doesn't feel very much loved, so he built up walls and focuses on his music. His father supports his music.

He is 20 years old now, in the conservatory. He wants to be independent from his father's help and financial assistance, who wants him to do what he could do in his youth…. He would say to him: "Son you can do whatever you want".

Music is the only thing that keeps his attention, the only thing he loves. He has a lot of pride in his appearance, bus is not very deep. He remembers his mother, knew that he would be separated from her, when he "signed up for it" before he was born. It was very painful though to not know his mother and only spend only a few days with her.

*<u>Death transition</u>: In his room, has some sort of disease... Cholera. Is alone, and is regretting not insisting on meeting his mother, and writing more music. Does not regret never being in love... he was too cold inside for that, but is at peace with it now.

Paul, mid 30's Native American man. August 2014

Life #1

Sees lights, gemstones….. shifting skin and hair colors. Is a white baby boy, with dark hair…… 2 years old now…. A part of himself was resisting coming into this existence, because it's so hard here…….. He is now holding his mother's hand, is happy, curious and innocent.

Matthew, early 40's European man. August 2014

Life #1

Is a woman, has poor raggedy clothes on. Is Dutch or French.... 1537-39, Holland. She has bad skin, people are making fun of her. She is in her 40's, has 1 child. She sells things for work. People are afraid of her, and are hating on her..... they think that she is a witch....... The officials are taking her away, tying her up.... They want her to confess to witchery. They torture her to death.

Life #2

Boy in India. 1 year old, born into a wealthy family. Has 4 siblings.

*Plus 15 years into the future: Is in a garden.... Playing, and being naughty..... prankish.... He is afeminite, gay maybe..... he likes the arts and nature. He got kicked in the balls for being too feminine. He has feelings for other men, and is heart-broken.

60 years old now, is unhappy..... he found happiness in helping and taking care of animals. His father and brothers are still alive. He never had to work. 1860's, in South India. His favorite thing is the simplicity, sharing, and his animals.

His advice: be happy, fully live your dreams.

*Death transition: Is by himself, at peace. Dying of old age.

Life #3

Man, 18 years old. Sees ships around, catching fish. He is strong and good looking. He is full of love, laughter and in good health. In Sweden or Denmark, 4 or 5 AD. Has a hard life, but a good life. He has a fiancé he loves. His biggest dream is to have a family with his fiancé and his own boat. He also loves the ocean and fishing, goes fishing one day on a ship in a storm...... was warned by an elderly person in the village to not go out into the storm.... But he didn't listen and went out anyway.... He ended up drowning as the whole ship went under water.

*(This is where I felt intuitively guided to change the course of his history, to stop him from going out fishing into the storm that day.... Because he was so young and full of life, and had a lot of potential still to be realized.....)

He is back at his parent's home now, decided to listen to the village elder and stay in that day. He stayed at home and did not go on the boat fishing. He evaded death that day.... And instead chose to live, and to work a lot, be a good husband and father, to listen to the elders and to tell stories. He promises to do good with his time and his life.

*<u>Death transition</u>: He is surrounded by his family and children…. They are all grown up. He is proud of them. His wife is by his side, holding his hand. He has a fever, is in his 60's. He is happy with his life, feels fulfilled and grateful to have lived so long.

Fred, mid 40's Hispanic man. August 2014

Life #1

Woman in a dress…. Wearing an elaborate gown. 20 years old, in a royal court in France in the 1500's. Her name is "Matilda Tergensen". There is an event, a dance…… She is betrothed to the prince or a member of the royal court. She is not happy, because it is an arranged marriage between families. She is refusing to get married. She gets shot in the stomach by her iancé, because she refuses to cooperate. The man wears an elaborate uniform…. He is humiliated, has a pistol with a ball. She is shocked, and feels robbed….. There is no consequence to him about this, about killing her.

She sees herself killing him in a previous life…..she understands the karmic retribution….. she is now freeing the karmic tie by forgiveness and release of anger in the stomach.

Life #2

Leather boots on, man in his mid 30's. Has a dark suit on…. There is lots of scientific equipment around, is in a laboratory. He is working with Nicola Tesla. His name is "Stewart", in the US in New York in the 1800's, away from the city….. His job is to "assist the wizard". It is kind of scary working with Nikola Tesla, because he has knowledge "from a higher realm" that he is not supposed to have.

There is a lot of pressure from outside forces, he is being watched, and has angered some powerful people... Tesla's inventions threaten to upset the order of things. He is starting to not feel safe working there. He is also a scientist, and believes in what Tesla is trying to do, which is wireless energy distribution. He has a family to support, and has received some threats too.... He has to leave working with Tesla, even though he is sad about it and doesn't want to go..........Tesla's work will soon be shut down, he sais that he "has a mission" but doesn't tell what it is, because people get frightened if they know too much too soon..... Tesla has the ability to talk to "Higher Beings". This technology could be weaponized..... Free energy is not going to happen in his lifetime.........Tesla's biggest vision is getting energy from up, not down.... Because it is destructive to the environment to get it from the earth...

Tesla goes on to work on other things, but is afraid to start something new. "They" tried to drive him insane. He died of a broken heart and poor. He does not want to come back to earth again.....

*Death transition: Stewart is lying in bed, dying of old age, in his 70's. His family and doctor are around him. He has a hard time breathing, is ready to go.

Myra, early 20's Caucasian woman, September 2014

Life #1

Brown shoes on. Young girl, 12 years old. There is a man with a hat on and other women there too, they are her friends. In Holland, Amsterdam, 1942. Her name is "Joselle" she is Dutch. She is looking for food, goes to school. She is not happy… she is lost…. Doesn't know where her home is…… She wants to be a teacher when she grows up.

*Plus 10 years into the future: In her house. She is married, has 1 child, a little girl. She is not working. Her husband is at work…..as a librarian. Her new last name is "Austrich" or "Auswich"…….She is missing from her life having a career. She doesn't feel safe where she lives because of a man, a neighbor who is lurking and watching her….. he rapes her one day……..(This is where I had her pray and ask for her angels to come and help/assist her. Forgiveness and self-love, release of trauma)

*Death transition: Her husband is there…. She has cancer, is 34 years old.

Life #2

Woman, with high heels on. 33 years old. Wearing a big, fancy dress. Her name is "Martha". She is in her room, in her house. In Virginia in 1752. She is married, but her

husband is on a ship going back to England for trade…..
he works in the cotton industry. They own a farm, but
there are no slaves working there……there are white
men picking the cotton. Other people have slaves on their
farms, but they don't want to support slavery so they
don't have any. She works, sells mittens. She is not happy
with her life…….she wants to travel, to learn and to be
free….. but it's not "proper" for a lady to do that in this
time. She has 1 child, a son…… wants to grow a garden….
Loves her son, home and family.

*Death transition: On a bed, has pneumonia. Her father,
mother, son and husband are all there. She is 70 years old.

Thomas, mid 20's Middle Eastern-American man. November 2014

Life #1

Has shoes on, they are made of fur. Man, is 23 years old. Sees nature and rocks all around….. he is out hunting, for wolves. He is all alone, his family died…… There are others in the tribe…. There is a girl he likes and her parents who are shamans…. Indigenous tribe, in Russian or Alaska…. There is snow, in the "Svareytal" region. The year is 1783. His name is "Shon". He likes being free and hunting, going on adventures. His family all died… he is scared to love again and to lose it….. he wants to marry that girl in the tribe and have a family and form a new tribe.

*10 years ahead in time: Is in the same place… married the girl in the tribe "Nicole" has a son, and they live in the same town. He is happy with his life, but still has a fear of losing them.

*Death transition: He is laying down on the ground…. His family is around him… his wife, son and daughter…. He feels their love and is releasing the fear of losing love.

Life #2

Man, is barefoot, 28 years old. His name is "Dani Sukana", he lives in Kauai, in 1912. He is swimming and diving in the ocean, fishing….. Has a wife and a baby, they are standing by the shore….. They are native Hawaiian, never left the island. He is happy and satisfied with his life, is a fisherman.

*Plus 10 years ahead in time: There's a fire in some houses, and there's invaders in the village…. White people are invading, they want to take over the land by force. He can't fight them, so they are running away to another spot in the jungle. He is not afraid…. He meets a shaman in the jungle by name of "Kahu"… he learns a lot from him…. How to speak to the Spirits of the land, through a special meditation. His family is with him, they are safe. He is fearless, he likes being that way.

*Death transition: He gets shot in the back, by white Americans. He was trying to fight back, to take back his land…. Is 50 years old. He was angry about it, but is at peace now… has forgiven them for killing him.

Life #3

Has pointy, weird-looking shoes on. Is 42 year old Chinese man. Lives in a town in China, in "Twa mee" in 1962. His name is "Son Yee". He sees other people around him, they are selling things on the street…. He is there to buy some food. He is a Daoist Master…. Has studied since he was 8 years old. He has no family, he was raised in a monastery….. his parents left him there because they couldn't take care of him…… he feels abandoned…..He is not supposed to get married……..he has only been in love from afar, in a Chinese woman he doesn't know, but feels love towards.

His advice: Breathe… take life one step at a time…. Anything can be accomplished. He wants to accomplish self-mastery, which is complete awareness of oneself.

He likes the tranquility he feels inside. Would like to experience love with that woman, but is choosing to stay at the monastery instead… because he has nothing if he leaves the monastery….

*Death transition: He is meditating and getting ready to pass on. Everyone in the village is there, including the woman he loves… he tells her loves her, and that he will see her again in another lifetime when they can be together.

Jose, Mid 30's Hispanic man.
December 2014

Life #1

Barefoot, or has thin sandals on..... Woman, thin, tall 20 years old named "Maria". There are other people around, part of a group, who are looking for spiritual answers and what they should do next. She wants to make everyone feel good and comfortable. In Italy or Greece, 300-400 AD. Her role: to keep going, to make sense of things, to be a leader and help others. It's hard for her, to hold onto things. She is not very happy with her life.... Her family is not around. She walked a long way to get here, and left her family behind. She wants to feel hope... but feels doubt and anxiety. She has faith in love... is in love now with someone, who she believes in. The best thing about her life is that people respect and admire her.

*Plus 20 years ahead in time: At home, in Europe somewhere. She speaks Roman, or Latin.... Feels alone, has no family.... Is surrounded by people who come to see her for some sort of message of hope. She tries to keep people around her together. The political situation of her country is that everything is up in the air.... She is losing hope in the future and is scared.... Love gives her faith.

*Death transition: On bed, people all around her, villagers and friends. She is dying of old age... has some regrets and feels very emotional.

Life #2

Man, 25-30 years old, has leather shoes on. His name is "Adam" (Walrick...?) He is trying to figure out a way to be influential: is a writer or a journalist... something political. In England, early 1800's (1820 or 1830). Has a wife.... Wants to be more in love with her and more connected to her... her name is "Mary"... she seems distant and lonely.

He wants more... keeps looking toward the future, not noticing the present. What makes him happy is being right, being followed by many and being listened to....it defines his self-worth. What he wants to achieve in life is to open up people's eyes to truth. He feels "truth", inside himself... but doesn't let people inside, into his heart, because he feels like a fraud, he feels so much pain and anguish inside. He wants power and recognition more than anything... wants to let go of false ambition and the need to be recognized. He feels like "he sold his soul to the devil" in this lifetime when he first became a man, because he wanted to have it all.... So he became selfish, and left everyone behind for that. He is not happy.... Happiness meaning being in love and that being enough, and not being afraid. He feels like he has a lot of letting go to do, of how he let others down. He learned: to forget about himself and care about others.... To be vulnerable... He doesn't like to be vulnerable, he likes to hide.

*Plus 20 years into the future: He is in a room... someone is taking care of him.... He is sick, with pneumonia. A nurse is taking care of him. His wife left him, she is not around. Has one child, a girl. He wants to die... because he feels like he failed, that he didn't live his truth and didn't focus on love. Is 55 years old.

Advice to himself: Be true to yourself. Don't get pulled in the wrong direction by the ego driven ambitions. Don't be afraid to show all of you. Put your dark side into the light. Get comfortable with who you are.

*Death transition: In a library or study. Dying of old age, around 70 years old. There is a nurse of a caretaker around, but she is cold and distant...

Emilia, 60 year old Caucasian woman. December 2014

Life #1

She went back into her own life, beginning at the age of 5 years old. Here she got to retrieve her earliest memories and work on releasing her earliest learned fears and emotional response patterns.

Life #2

Woman in her 20's, but feels much older. She has no shoes and rags on, because she is very poor. She is brown skinned, African.....somewhere in an African village.... She has a baby in her arms, and another one at her feet. Everything is an effort for her, and there is dust everywhere.... No water.... It's hot and dry and dusty, there is never enough water. She is not educated, has no sense of time, and doesn't even know how old she is exactly. She doesn't have a husband, and doesn't know whose children they are. She was always there in her village.... There are people around, but she feels no connection with them or anyone particularly... she lives on the outskirts of the village. She is deaf, doesn't work, and is barely surviving.... Even walking is an effort and painful.

*10 years back in time: She is by a hut, it's dusty. It's her home, she is playing with other children. Her mother is inside. She is a happy child, likes to skip and play. Eats a green mush porridge… bananas and greens. Her father is in the village.

*Forward ahead in time: She is deaf and isolated. Has a sarong on and a bucket of water on her head. She didn't choose this lifetime, this was like a penance… a punishment or here to learn lessons. The lesson of this lifetime: gratitude, for being alive. She learned to be grateful for life, but "being different" is hard. Being poor, hot and thirsty all the time is hard. She is experiencing something hard right now, to gain gratitude. She feels bad that she can't take care of her children, hopes that they will survive somehow…

*She is now going back to the previous life before this one, to see why she came into this life:

In that life she was white and privileged…. She had a sense of knowing that she is ok, had a sense of community… but was not grateful enough for what she had. She had to come back to experience the opposite, to know and learn gratitude and the sense of being accepted by the village friends, by first knowing what it feels like to be unaccepted.

*Death transition: She is on the ground, by herself. Her children are dead because she couldn't take care of them. She is dehydrated and hungry…. All bones and hopeless… she is grateful for her children, but feels a sense of loss and remorse, that she couldn't take care of them. Slips away quietly and alone.

Melanie, Hispanic Mix middle aged woman. January 2015

Life #1

Browns shoes on, wears an old frock. Woman, 17 years old. Is in a village, in Eastern Europe… near Prague in 1810. She is carrying water and makes milk products. She lives with her parents and sisters. Her name is "Tasha" or "Anastasia". She is very poor, lives in a shack with dirt floors and stone walls, but she wants to escape that and daydreams of being a Queen.

*Plus 10 years ahead in time: She is with a man, he is her husband. She is in love with him, his name is "Marco", he is Sicilian. She met him in her village, fell in love and moved away with him. Now she doesn't work, lives in a home with lots of green and open areas. The best thing about her life is that she is happy, content and is loved and taken care of.

*Death transition: She is in bed, she is 76 years old and is dying of old age. She is happy with her life and her family is there with her. She learned in this lifetime: she focused on having the life she always wanted and got it, and it was effortless.

Life #2

Body is covered in heavy stuff.. jewelry and robes. Lots of gold. She is a woman, and her gown is made of gold. Her name is "Naala", she is 16 years old and she lives in Egypt. Her father is a big, powerful king... she is afraid of him because he is very strict with her. She has brothers and sisters, but her mother is not around. Time is unknown, but is in ancient times... pyramids are around. She sees a lot of outdoor areas, lakes and smooth stones. She is very well educated, can read and write hieroglyphs and do math. Her position is to be married off. There are a lot of big parties and festive events, and she likes them.... She feels powerful... she conducts ceremonies and her opinion matters. She is connected to everything mystical, the gods in the sky, the earth, temples and stones... she is being honored and revered, in a ceremony now... feels powerful. She has a lot of head things and comfortable clothing on, in a ritual.. she feels good, protected and safe, free to adorn herself and connect to the gods. She is invoking the gods in a ritual, has hands in the air... sees the altars, there is alchemy. She is connected to nature, and to a lot of gods.

*Death transition: She is being killed by a bunch of villagers, men. Her arms are spread out... she is being killed by drowning. It feels like a revolt or revolution, not anything personal to her. She is 23 years old... feels oddly peaceful... is fighting it, but doesn't feel any anger really in her heart.

Raphael, late 20's Mixed Nationality man, March 2015

Life #1

Leather strappy sandals on feet. Man, "Michael" in his late 20's, white Middle Eastern or European. He is alone, walking outside in nature, in the mountains. In Europe or somewhere in the Middle East. Ancient times, 1600's or earlier. He is a warrior, is a strong warrior-guardian advisor and leader.... Connected to the community of higher echelon of decision makers. His family is around in a village area. He is happy with his life, but there is heaviness, a sort of big responsibility that he carries. He feels strong and empowered and peaceful, being of service.... Almost like a stoic nature of care for the greater good of the people. He had to be a warrior. He has a responsibility of keeping the village safe.... Is happy, but also always on guard with maintaining the peace.

*Plus 10 years ahead in time: He is in a warm and friendly environment with a beautiful family. Has 3 children and is in love with his wife "Melody". There is a beautiful content and fullness in this life.

*Death transition: He is laying on a bed, surrounded by his family, sharing lots of love. He is 100+ years old, dying of old age.

Life #2

Barefoot… 30 year old woman "Belle Krungpen (spelling…?)".. She is by herself, but there are other women nearby, her friends.

She is taking a bath in the outdoor bathtub that's part of the house. Her body feels smooth, beautiful and healthy. She is not married, because she is interested in other women, a lesbian. In ancient Roman times. She is part Roman, part Persian. She basks in the glory of her sensual nature, doesn't involve herself too much in the outside world.

She feels really good and relaxed in her world and life, has no stress. There is lots of opulence, beauty and abundance. She wants to show people how soft, beautiful and powerful life can be. The purpose of this lifetime: artistic expression shared with the outside world….. a muse to many artists. She wants to experience more people opening themselves up to beauty and bliss… beauty is her legacy.

*Death transition: in the forest, she was shot by an arrow by a manly beastly man character, on purpose because he was threatened by her beauty and freedom. He is her older brother. She is 38 years old. Forgives him for killing her, because she has so much love for people who don't understand. She has no regrets.

Leanna, 50 year old Caucasian woman. March 2015

Life #1

20 year old woman… in pre-historic times. She is by herself, in the jungle, there is clear blue sky above… She is happy & content. There are other people around, but no one near her now. She lives in a cave… communicates by thought…. Eats fruits, berries and plants. She is not afraid of anything. There are dinosaurs there, in the distance. She has children, back in the cave.

*Plus 20 years into the future: She is on the same field just older. Her body feels fragile.. it's cold out, she is wearing heavy furs. Her family is dead or gone.

The purpose of this incarnation: to bring light where there is none, with advanced thought, advanced ideas and by escaping the rigors of difficult life.

*Death transition: She doesn't want to die… Is sitting, and knows she is dying. There are shadows around her, she is not sure if she is alone dying of old age… she doesn't want to go, because she wants life and is scared of death and the afterlife.

Life #2

Woman, 16 years old, "Michelle". In France in 1620. She is a peasant girl, in a dirty village, trapped in a tiny narrow life, with mediocre thoughts and people. She doesn't feel like she belongs there...keeps saying : "This is not fair.. not the truth..."

She is not doing what she is supposed to be doing... she is treading in mud, carrying a yolk with milk, walking in the dirt and mud. She doesn't like anything about her life... She does love her family and they love her. Her mother is someone she recognizes as her someone in her life today.

The purpose of this life: to shine light...her kindness and her love is her gift to others.

*Plus 10 years ahead in time: She is in the same village. Had children, but they are dead. She is not married, and feels alone. She sees around her a dark energy ring, that no one can penetrate... she wants this removed to be free of it. But she is scared to release, because it's her protection, her wall of defense.. because it's all she has.

*Plus 10 more years in time: She is in the same village. She is now a scientist... working and researching and it's a beautiful day out. She learned to love and accept herself.

*Death transition: 40 years old... in her study... a man comes in and lights her office on fire... there are angry people wanting her gone... She forgives them for this, and then releases the body.

Frank, late 20's Caucasian man, March 2015.

Life #1

Man in his mid 30's named "Thomas". Has a hat on, is alone. In Prescott, in the Southwest USA. He is not married, his family is in the mountains. He moves hay for work. His favorite part of life: freedom. His life purpose: enjoy life while surviving. Does not want to have a family, he is happy by himself. He loves walking through forests.

*Death transition: He is sad that he is alone and no one knows who he is. In his 70's. Dying of old age and sadness, his head hurts from something. Regrets not embracing love or connecting with other people. He had a lot of pain because his dad used to beat him when he was little… it's why he left home.

Life #2

Man in his mid 20's named "James Thorton". He is on a Navy ship, working as a mid ship man, doing daily tasks in the middle of the ocean. On a big steal ship… he likes to work. It's in the 1940's, and he is en route to Korea… to bomb people. He was forced to be here, by his family and society… he feels really bad about it, and cries a lot because of his guilt of bombing people…. He is in charge of placing bombs. Part of WWII.

*One year later: He is married to "Katherine Jameson" (spelling...?) from Florida. He loves her family. He came back to San Diego after his trip to Korea and met here there. They are very happy and in love, but they don't have children because she can't have children.

*<u>Plus 5 years ahead in time</u>: He is working at a car factory. Wants to be a writer, to write stories about his adventures. His stories will be made into movies by him... One of the biggest ones is called "Captain America". He published his stories through Marvel. He loves doing that and is happy about that. Is excited about creating Captain America. He has no children though, and is sad about it because he wanted to....

*<u>Death transition</u>: He is with his wife. In his 80's. They are still really happy. In 1975 they pass away together, as a choice. She was his soul mate and he loved her very much. (He wants to find her again in this lifetime after he got reminded of this great love).

Life #3

Woman, in her 60's named "Vida". In Senegal in the 1800's. She lives in a village... a beautiful paradise. She is the village teacher, teaches wisdom. She is happy with her life, and her body feels good, she is very peaceful. She takes a lot of walks, and communes with flowers. She loves making tea for people, communing with them and loving them. She has no regrets, and no children because the man she was with left her and broke her heart... she forgave him and herself, but never really healed from that or has allowed herself to fall in love with another man since.

Her advice: "Forgiveness within the soul heals Eternity"

*<u>Death transition</u>: She is inside, looking at the sun through the windows. She feels young, but her body is really old. She chooses to die, to leave her body.

James, 30 year old mixed ethnicity man. April 2015

Life #1

Man, naked. He is by a waterfall somewhere in Europe. Woman by his side, his wife named "Isabelle". He is holding a big stick, not sure what year it is, there is no track record of time…. They live in caves, wear furs and skins. It's so hot outside that he is not wearing much. Their language is: talking around the fire and draw pictures on the walls of the caves. He is a serious guy, feels serious because he is protecting a lot of people, because they are all so confused. He talks to them, explaining things… about what they can or can't do…. A way-shower. He explains beliefs about lots of gods and how they rule them. He believes in chaos.

*Death transition: In the forest, 10 years older than before. A panther bit his face off. He doesn't feel anything, because he doesn't mind this happening… it is all part of nature eating and feeding itself.

Life #2

Man, on a big stage. There are thousands of people, watching him. He plays the guitar, for everyone. Is in a band called "The Jimi Hendrix Experience". His name is "Jimi Hendrix". He is 49 years old, but feels like 20. Love is his inspiration for music, he is deeply in love with music. He feels every cell in his body is exploding, his heart explodes when he plays. His favorite song he wrote is "Purple Haze". He doesn't really care for art forms, just the art.... Doesn't really care about other artists and comparing himself to them. He doesn't have children, doesn't want to. He was never married, but has been with 2 women he felt like he was married to... "Jesse Justin"...

He does a lot of drugs, smokes a lot of weed... His message to the world is: Presence and love. Just be who you are.. no bullshit" Playing the guitar feels fun.

*<u>Death transition</u>: 69 years old, dying of doing too many drugs... heroin, painkillers, weed, alcohol. He is doing all of this because he doesn't want to live anymore... he feels empty and had a lot of loss that he can't let go of the pain in his heart... Died in 1962. His advice: It doesn't have to hurt so bad.. the loss of family, friends, women...

Dennis, Caucasian male in his early 40's. April 2015

Life #1

Both man and woman, young. …. Is dancing in a free space. On an earthly planet… feels familiar. Feels really big… big energy…. Feels so much love… feels the roots of the trees…. The purpose of this existence is to be everything and to be free. Happening sometime in the future, in 2055. Sees the mountains and the ocean. Crystals under his/her feet… is here but also flying around. Flying over Los Angeles….sees it as a glowing ball of light. The true essence of this city shining through….. Harmony and collaboration. Lemurian pearl essence…. The ocean came and washed everything away in 2022. There was an earthquake in 2016 and 2019…. One in North Los Angeles close to San Francisco and the other one closer to Los Angeles, of a big magnitude, where a lot of people died… thousands. There was a great purification on earth, through an increase in population. There were too many people, had to be a purification…

Some people died through anger, ego, power, war, from the disconnect of the planet's pure energy & food. Only a few million of people are left on this planet.

2016/2017: So much discord…. Sees beauty, feels a lot of energy (challenging, suffering and loving). To transmute the negative, you have to reconnect to Source and be more and more in alignment, to be in balance and equilibrium.

He/she is going back now to the mountains and the water. Goes to where the pure energy is. Feels everything very intimately. He/she is an angel, comes from a Supernova and doesn't have a name…. is not important. Is here to balance out the masculine and feminine energy.

Advice: Connect to your purest power. We need you. Trust". He/she has wings… feathers, are big and physical. The rays of his/her being fragment into form as human or animal. Animals are the purest beings, especially nature. The form he/she takes shape most is an owl.

Message to humanity at this time: dance, return to your center, slow down, be closer to nature more often, because urban environments deplete people of their natural power.

Now he/she is spinning around Saturn, all the rings around have the rings/energy that he/she carries…. Is now taking this energy and giving it to planet earth for rebalance.

Our purpose is to harmonize and expand on the love and light. People are close now to age-less-ness. Time is less of a need and more of a necessity. As technology has evolved we have to go back to nature, re-focus and re-balance. The dangerous man-made equipment and pollution has shifted. We have to reconnect to Source Energy, that's what our purpose is. We have the connection to take different forms, but are always connected to the celestial apex….. "I am everything"…..55 others have this capability now, they come and go… we all know each other. Sometimes they leave and then all come back. The reason to embody into human form is to experience love in the physical, this is the only reason why we are here!.... We reconnect Source energy when we connect with each other. In homosexuals there is still a balancing discord. There is too much shame and fear in people.

Now he/she is full spectrum rainbow white light. Out of form he/she can re-materialize into one body (animal or human) and all of this light and sensitivity remains.

Balancing all the planets together is also very important. These planets move a lot, like a pendulum. In & out.... There is a Planet X coming around earth's orbit... pillars as an anchor of light and energy. There is another one called Planet O.

He/she is in Egypt now.... The place that's closest to his/her resonance. In 111 BC we were both embodied there together (meaning myself, the Hypnotherapist). There were pyramids back then, they rose through the earth. There were people and greater forces and sources that were involved with creating the pyramids. They were built by the consciousness of the awakened ones at that time, that made them physically manifest. There were alien hybrids.

Patty, Asian mid 20's woman.
June 2015

Life #1

Barefoot... 23 year old woman, "Kellie". She is standing by herself... There are brown rocks all around, red inside each rock. Her family is dead... they got killed. She was drawn to this place... looks like planet Mars, called "Grolthas". The planet is dying/being destroyed.... She is not supposed to be there anymore. She has no food or water... is dying.

The lesson from this lifetime: "No matter what happens, keep going. Even when all seems to be lost"

Life #2

Woman, "Lani" who is 20 years old.... has a dress and Moccasins on. There are people far away from her... She is near water. The place is called Lemuria... everything is blue. She lives on her own, and does energy healings in her home.... People come to her, she heals with her hands and crystals. She was born with this gift, and she likes it. She is not married, and she doesn't want to. She likes being by herself and with others, she belongs to the people and not to anyone specifically, she doesn't want children or a family, is happy with her life.

Her parents are in the village. There are pyramids on the planet, on the mountains.. they are big... their purpose is to heal people and transport them… you go inside and they are portals taking people to somewhere else… to other planets… people leave physically and their soul partially. The pyramids are made of stones, of granite, and are found in North America, close to Hawaii… one has to take a boat there. Also in lower North America, by the shore.

Technology: they use the energy between their hands, and magnetics. They are a peaceful society… they go up to the temples and pray to "The all that is"… they eat vegetarian foods, not animals… they respect them because they are a part of them. There is no money exchange, no need for it, because everyone helps each other.

Her favorite thing about this life: peace, being able to help others… we are all one. Also, she has a shiny sphere, she looks at it and is around it, it charges her up…. It comes from "God", is made of love and light… helps everyone… looks like a lightning and always spins…

People live as long as they want to.. they can leave (die) anytime. People don't experience physical pain, it's energetic pain… they have to release it to heal…. Their bodies are different anatomically.

*Death transition: She is outside. Something happened… something heavy and negative that wants them to go.. she can feel it… It's a dark energy… it changes everything, it's coming from everywhere… it's a force, heavy and new. They have to leave through the temples, to a different planet. She doesn't want to leave…. But has to… she leaves her physical body behind and goes. The energy is

74

similar to the previous planet's in destructiveness.. this is happening because of "ego" power and control... the ones who want them to leave are negative beings, some are from Earth, some are from other planets.

She chose to come back to earth because she is not done learning. She wants and needs to challenge herself more and learn other lessons... to learn to love everyone.

The purpose of her life here now is to help others more, to learn gratitude.

Her advice: all is not lost... you can keep going!

John, Middle aged mixed ethnicity man. June 2015

Life #1

Man, going through the jungle.. in Viet Nam. Is with other people there… He is an 18 year old soldier, his is name is "Jerol Figueroa". He is Hispanic, lives in the US.

It's 1969. He didn't choose to go to war, but was drafted.. he didn't have anywhere else to go… is mad about it, he didn't want to go to war…He has been there for 6 months, killed 4 Viet cong people, and is really sad about it. He hasn't been injured yet…. Wants to go home… He want to be at home playing music on his guitar, Rock n Roll…

His dream is to be a rock star, like Jimi Hendrix. He wants to help people understand about how the war is… bad!!!

He will die soon, in a month.

His legacy: is to die in the muck of the war.

His advice: be yourself, don't wait to tell the people you love that you love them… life is precious. So much beauty, and horror in this life… it's all the same… pain and pleasure… there are moments when there is peace at night… then the shooting starts and it all gets dissolved… this life is a paradox.

*Death transition: In the jungle in the water…. "They are closing down on us… Charlie got us pinned in…."

Life #2

Man, 19 years old. He has sandals on and armor. He is there with his brothers, walking through the forest "Kurukshetra" in India. His name is "Arjun Shishodia". His mission is to restore the world's dharma. His father and mother are in the palace, Krishanku, in the North-East region of India. The year is 3,000 BC.

He wants to restore dharma, by killing his cousins, because they are ignorant and greedy and selfish. His duty is to kill them… he doesn't want to, but has to. "Lord Krishna" told him to do this, by touching him on the forehead.. he is a tall and beautiful Being…

His favorite thing to do is to be with his brothers and to shoot his bow and arrow… he is the greatest at it… people cheer him on.

He is in love, she is in the palace and he wants to marry her. His family is wealthy, but his brother will lose everything through playing dice. He is angry at him because of this, but loves and respects him very much.

*Plus 20 years: In a camp… there are tents and army people… they are in a war… "the greatest war of all time "Mahabharata". His role in it is being a general. He has killed tens of thousands of people… this is his dharma. It makes him feel exhilarated and sad, angry and heavy-hearted… He is at war because they killed his son who was 22 years old, so now he is taking revenge.

He has 21 more years to live…. Enjoys his life, but regrets killing so many people…he knows that he will have to atone for killing so many people… is not afraid though, because there is no death…

*Death transition: He is on a mountain, 85 years old. He is dying of old age.. his brothers are around him, his wife is gone. He regrets not having his son "Aviman" for longer…

His advice: love, trust, persevere, hold fast to Krishna, he is the truth. This life is a dream…

Elizabeth, Middle-aged Caucasian woman. June 2015

Life #1

A 13 year old girl, barefoot in the woods. In a pink dress, with a stick in her hand. She is by herself, looking for something.... Leaning on a tree on the ground, she is tired or sad. Her name is "Lee", she is American. She is in a big forest, there is water close by... she might be lost.. she walked a lot, her home is far away... Her parents are dead, they were killed in a fire. The year is 1802. She is not in school, she has never been. Her family is medium/average well-off. She wants to be an explorer when she grows up. Her feet hurt from walking. After walking for 3 days, she found water by a river, her dress has tears in it, she built a small tent by herself, she eats fish from the river...

*Plus 10 years: In a wagon, driving and looking out... it's hot and dusty. She is going to someone's house or job. Has a hat and light blue pants on, and shirt. For work she looks for odd things, searches articles in the woods, deserts and water. She is wearing a safari hat, shoes on and is in Serbia now.... Looking for a horse for her job. She wants to find a new family, people she can spend time with whom she likes. She doesn't speak much because she can't hear very well. She writes on a pad she keeps with her... about her parents, where she is going and about her travels.

*Plus 10 years: She is lying down on a truck on a bed... she is sick.. no one knows why... there are lots of windows that she can see out of, and is not afraid. She is married now, to someone named "John" who is far away. Her daughter is with her in the truck "Gail Potter". She loves her job, daughter and horse, and wishes she saw her husband more often. She travels so much, with her daughter in Europe… they are in Italy now. The horse's name is "Peter.

She found a very special and rare tree in the forest… it is special and unique because of its bark and leaves…. There is a certain oil in the bark that when you chip it and eat it, it can heal you and make you well from any disease. It is called the "Pompas" tree, and it helps heal people who are dying. It is in the woods where she was in the US in the South. Many people know about this tree, and they chopped it down to make medicine out of it… now there is no more of it left. She has some of it in her bag, in case her daughter gets sick….

*Death transition: She is on a farm, lying on top of her horse, she is crying because he is dead. Her daughter is there with a glass of water, crying.. She is 80 years old, her horse was 20 years old. She is dying of sadness. The horse is her father's spirit, reincarnated as a horse. Her daughter is her mother. The small boy who delivers hay, 7 years old, is her (current day) friend.

Life #2

*Future-life Progression:

Her name is "Flora" and she is wearing high heels, kneeling down. Her daughter "Zooline" is with her. She is in outer space, on a spaceship. She is worried that she won't see her husband "Jett "again... they have 2 children.

The year is 3,000 AD. Her daughter is trying to fix the spaceship, she is kneeling down on the floor... she feels calm... they are trying to find a rare planet... they are looking for it, it's a half planet half star. They can't seem to land on it, because it sends the spaceship out of orbit, pushes it away. There is one other person on board, wearing white... making food in another room... (she recognizes him as someone from her current life today). He helps them stabilize and fix the spaceship. Her partner is on Earth.. it is a very empty planet now, is missing a lot of people and the water, because people used it up and it was taken away by Beings from other planets.

The people who are left on Earth are fighting to save the planet's resources and people from another planet, who are taking the resources away. The planet they are trying to land on is inhabited by small animals, similar to squirrels. She studied this planet, and discovered it herself. It took them a month to get to this planet. They travel via spaceship... they have small computers, small telescopes and other technological gadgets. Some friends and her husband built it.

*Death transition: She is inside a small spaceship, a small bubble/pod. She is sick... they are sending her off to die, in space, by herself. She is 53 years old. She is dying of cancer, brain cancer. She feels sad to leave her child and Michael... who she became very close to. She is confused as to why her husband left her to die in space... He was greedy with the water and food resources, he didn't want to share them... She couldn't talk to him before her death. She did land on the planet, for 10 minutes, only to see the animals and to experience it with her daughter.

Frederico, Early 40's Hispanic man. June 2015

Life #1

Man, 900 years old or more. He is by himself... known as "the One from the Sea"... Lives around Crete. The year is 18,000 BC. He is in and by the ocean, contemplating how beautiful it is. He is involved with community, arts and science. Lives in a large city not too far. He is visiting "Minoa" from the other side of the globe, a place known as "Atlantis". He was sent there as an emissary... there is something there that he needs to resolve with this side of the world... he came here to warn them about a catastrophe they will suffer.... This was seen by the "Oracles of Atlantis" in liquid crystals and the interpretation of them by certain priests in 200 years from that time.

The purpose of this life is to prepare the world of the coming change. The world as we know it is coming to an end. The entire planet will be wiped out... not everyone will die... Mother Earth will choose the ones she wishes to live.

He knows that he is infinite... feels all his incarnations....

Life #2

Woman, 27 years old. She is with other people... part of a caravan, they are moving through the jungle... between

Mexico and Guatemala. She is carried by a carriage… Her name is "Amaya". The year is 789 AD. They are traveling towards another city, has a message with her that she needs to deliver to "Jalan Pakkal", known as "the greatest of all kings". The message is: some of their women have been having dreams by the "gods from the sky". She is not married. There is an urgency that is preoccupying her mind right now.…

The king will start to make preparations for the extraterrestrial visit. She will see this, in 22 days. She felt tremendous joy and great celebration… the "visitors" are here, and they are wearing amazing costumes… they are very very large… white skinned, dark haired, 30 feet tall, look like humans. They are here to check up on them and are fleeing from something. King "Jalan" communicates with them telepathically. She is being asked to go with them… goes inside a spaceship.… It is big and beautiful inside. Seems so familiar to her somehow… she is not afraid… she was born there on it. She was created from earthling DNA but conceived and birthed on the spaceship. The purpose of this life: she was supposed to learn as much as she could on earth… she must return now to be a teacher, to the new children being born. They are orbiting the earth.She is seeing the giants on the spaceship, which is as big as a city.

*Death transition: She is by a waterfall.… In a cenote… on earth. She is 97 years old. Feels happy… There are a few other humans there. She has 2 children… they are there. She has a companion, but is not married, he is not there.… She passes on…

Diana, Early 40's Caucasian woman. June 2015

Life #1

Woman, has no shoes on. She is dancing… there are other people around. Inside a building, it is a happy occasion. Her family is there with her, her sisters and her brother, dad and mom. Her name is "Izula", she is Indian, from North India in 526 AD. She is happy with her life, she is young but not married. She wants to be a dancer when she grows up.

*Plus 10 years into the future: She is in a temple, illustrating a book, drawing people and flowers… it is a story of love, called "Hakashakarenga". She has a partner, "Iranga" but they are not married, because they don't believe in marriage, only in love. (She now recognizes the partner as a good friend from her present lifetime).

*Death transition: She is in a bed, with flowers all around her. She is very old, dying of old age. Her daughter, son and partner are there around her. She is sad because she doesn't want to leave him alone…

Life #2

Little boy, 9 years old. He has no shoes on, and no clothes on and is by himself. His name is "Shack", he is of Shibu nationality, is in South America. He lives in the forest with his family in a house made of grass. There is kind of a village close by, and a kind of school. His father likes to laugh a lot. He has siblings, a little sister and baby brother. He is in the forest, and now some people come there to teach them... how to use their mind. These people are alien hybrids, but are benevolent. They want to know about the nature medicines of the forest. They need the medicine to heal their people, who don't have oxygen. They communicate telepathically, and are controlling their minds to harvest medicine for them, from the leaves of the special trees. They are taking Ayahuasca, and are interested in a small leaf, which glows in the dark. There is a tree that glows at night, called the "Unka" tree. This tree has special healing abilities, it repairs tissues in the human body. The Beings put something inside of him, to monitor him and to collect information.

*Plus 10 years ahead in time: He is by the ocean, it is blue. It is somewhere else, on another planet... the moon looks a lot bigger. The Beings put him there, to monitor him and use his blood for transfusions, because his blood type is special. He is there with his wife and baby. He went on one of their spaceships, it was both scary and exciting. His wife and baby came with him on the spaceship. He is kept isolated. They eat corn, berries, yucca plants.. It is very beautiful there, but he is isolated and feels lonely. They are doing experiments about mental thinking, and are feeding them the special tree's leaves, to expand their consciousness. They come from far away, from the "Plato" galaxy. They are called "The Watchers" and they wish to help humanity, and are watching them, us, like watching a t.v show. We are fun for them, like entertainment.

They give us problems, or challenges, to see how we solve them. They are always watching us. They are not interfering with our lives, just adding to it. Like life challenges, to see how we develop and what works. They are now sending us crop circles and communicating to us that way. They are our creators. It was a collaboration with another planet's inhabitants. They programmed our DNA, and everything, with an open-circuit programming for things to enter. They watch us like we watch the Olympics… they laugh at us. They can interfere only very little, and they have been trying to help us to solve our problems. We can get in contact with them telepathically. They know everything! We have a choice, everything is a choice… the only choice we don't have is that they are watching us. They laugh at our stupidity. They don't like what is going on with the animals and all the torture of them and the animal factory farming. They have teams, and are betting on us like we do on sports teams.

The Jewish people are "the Chosen Ones" because they communicated with their watchers. The different races on planet Earth are coordinated by different planets, so they can identify us.

Drugs were given to us like the eggs in an Easter egg hunt… they were hid away, as a cheating device for quicker acceleration of consciousness. We as humans are here for their entertainment, but those who excel fast in this life are released from here, to go to the next level, like in the movie "The Hunger Games". Forming teams is helpful for elevation of levels. Those who rise quickly are ultimately released to freedom. It is a form of Enlightenment, it is based on Consciousness and happiness. "Winners win based on happiness". Those who are able to navigate the challenges with peace of mind WIN!

The "maya" of illusion is like a layer of fog that surrounds and distracts us. Winning is based on happiness. They want to see if we see through the fog to the truth. Only the happy survive. They are laughing at struggle... because it is not real. In some way though, they made misery enjoyable because there is a physical chemical rush that happens in the body, which is like a rush of endorphins. It is a trick... because we there is a chemical addiction in the body when we fail at something or are in pain. There is some pleasure in the pain, it is a sort of drug that the body creates...

We are a scientific and art experiment to them. They are highly proud of us, but are also frustrated with us because we are "stuck".... They gave the Mayans a timeline and a calendar for certain goals to be achieved. They didn't pass it... they were distracted and it stopped their movement for long periods of time. They took the Mayans away, for experiments and for blood... to make more humans. The Atlanteans were also moved away, and people from North Italy, the North Pole, Antarctica, China and Japan.

They built the pyramids, with anti-gravity magnetic force created by their minds.

We have a magic wand to make things happen, by our spoken words, saying "It is done" "And so it is" after visualizing and sending out thought intentions.

There are many other planets like Earth. We are slower than they anticipated, so they turned their focus away from us to other planets, because we are boring to them.... But we are now picking up momentum. Some of the people on earth now have been more successful at the "maya", the mirage, and getting out of it. They are the tricksters, they are successful. Crop circles are messages coming through from them, and through the media, and through some people such as "Bashar", "Marianne Williamson", "Desmond Tutu", "Nelson Mandela" and "Carmen Miranda".

We need to listen to the clues and signs, they are messages for us. We are given clues every day. We must work in teams for acceleration. We have to form trusting bonds. Built into "the game" is extra points for trusting each other and working together. Trust! for only one individual to rise alone, but to rise in a trust unity, to higher levels of evolution. Humans are magnetic... We pull those around us in the direction we are going. The power becomes greater in numbers, we increase the Forcefield.

Money is ok, it is fine. It is also a trap, people need to stop worrying and thinking so much about it.

Everything that brings you joy and pleasure without doing harm to another being is fine. It is a great disgrace to the Watchers that there are so many atrocities happening in the Middle East and Asia, especially that have to do with demeaning and hurting women. The holding down and control of women is based on fear of change. The Watchers did not anticipate the male ego to be holding down the entire race... it took a turn that was not anticipated... It happened through a challenge that was given to us, but it became a threat to the evolution of humanity because it divided the human race, even more than color or race has. They are always thinking of ways to challenge us. To the Watchers, our failures are both amusing and saddening.

To break free from the "maya" we must form healing retreats such as the Ayahuasca retreats in Peru and all over America, they are one key to breaking free, another key is music festivals. These guide us into ourselves and into happiness.

Corporate entities distract us, giving us false happiness. We are electrical units, and when we go into big corporate buildings like malls for example, we plug into that synthetic electricity grid, and we get plugged in like a computer. Malls are like a fan, giving us fake wind, which cools us temporarily but is not real wind.

Nature is real happiness, we get recalibrated in nature and need it... especially feeling the earth under our feet. We also need to find other seekers and like-minded people. The Watchers are hopeful. The worst thing that could happen already happened, but there is one more thing that could destroy us, is humans building artificial intelligence as human robots, because this is humans with lower consciousness trying to be like the Watchers.

Animals were given intelligence and intuition, with an inability to communicate with other species. They were planted here for their own evolution. A human soul can enter an animal body for their own evolution, and many do. What humans are doing to them in terms of factory farming and all the torture is not fair to the animals. All things that are alive have a soul. All souls are equal. All souls are equal. ALL SOULS ARE EQUAL.

Karma is a human idea. There is no karma, except for a desire for evolution. We have free choice, however we are choosing collectively, so others' free choices are interfering with ours.

God is all. God is the electrical current that is connecting us all together, running through us.

Life on Earth will not continue to go on forever... because of resources. The planet will need to be cleansed. They will clean it. They are part of the Annunaki, some are a part of it. The prototype of humanity is designed by the same team, from different planets and galaxies. Each put their people here for observation. Ultimately we are here for evolution and winning. Winning means collective happiness. Clarity of thinking is important, and clean minds, clean bodies, clean terrains because we are made of that.

In about 20 years there will be another big cleansing, by heat and water. From September 23rd 2015. Some will survive, but not many. The ones to survive are the ones who choose to and work for it. "We are all the chosen ones", we have to choose it for ourselves. Some will leave by spaceship, some will stay.

The most important information: Survival is based on collective evolution. Now we are evolving at a relative slow pace... When we evolve in groups, it's the ultimate way to switch levels. At this point we are all on similar levels. As long as one human sees another human beneath them or as not equal, they continue to be in the "maya". This is a team sport, it is designed this way specifically. Most people who are on a higher level as channels are not "better" than the others, they are just an open source for the greater good. We must all go together. "Never leave a man down". We always should go back and save others, throw them a life-line. When you are doing good, you must help others who are ready to move up!

We stand on the mountain and extend a hand to each other, to the others down below.

Revere nature, because without nature we could not exist. Wiping out the trees and animals is detrimental to our evolution. Have your focus be on the present and on nature. Social Media is an imprint of happiness, but it's like a mall… The World Wide Web helps us to disseminate information, but it is a web and we are all caught in it. Most things that have positives have negatives as well. For example, sugary soda tastes good, but is not good for your health.

The Watchers are observing all of this, it is very amusing to them. Their message: "Don't dismay. You all agreed to this, this was an agreement. All souls agreed to come here. Have less fear, and more fun and you will find the way out."

All the things that we are losing at right now, we are also winning by learning. If we destroy Earth, we will be moved to another planet. Have more fun… humor is helpful. When we are laughing we can open our minds to creativity to help humanity evolve. Humor unlocks and opens doors in the human brain, in the mind, so new ideas can come in through those doors. Humor unlocks, builds and opens. Children come to earth with infinite amounts of humor, we can learn so much from them.

*End of transmission here.

Printed in the United States
By Bookmasters